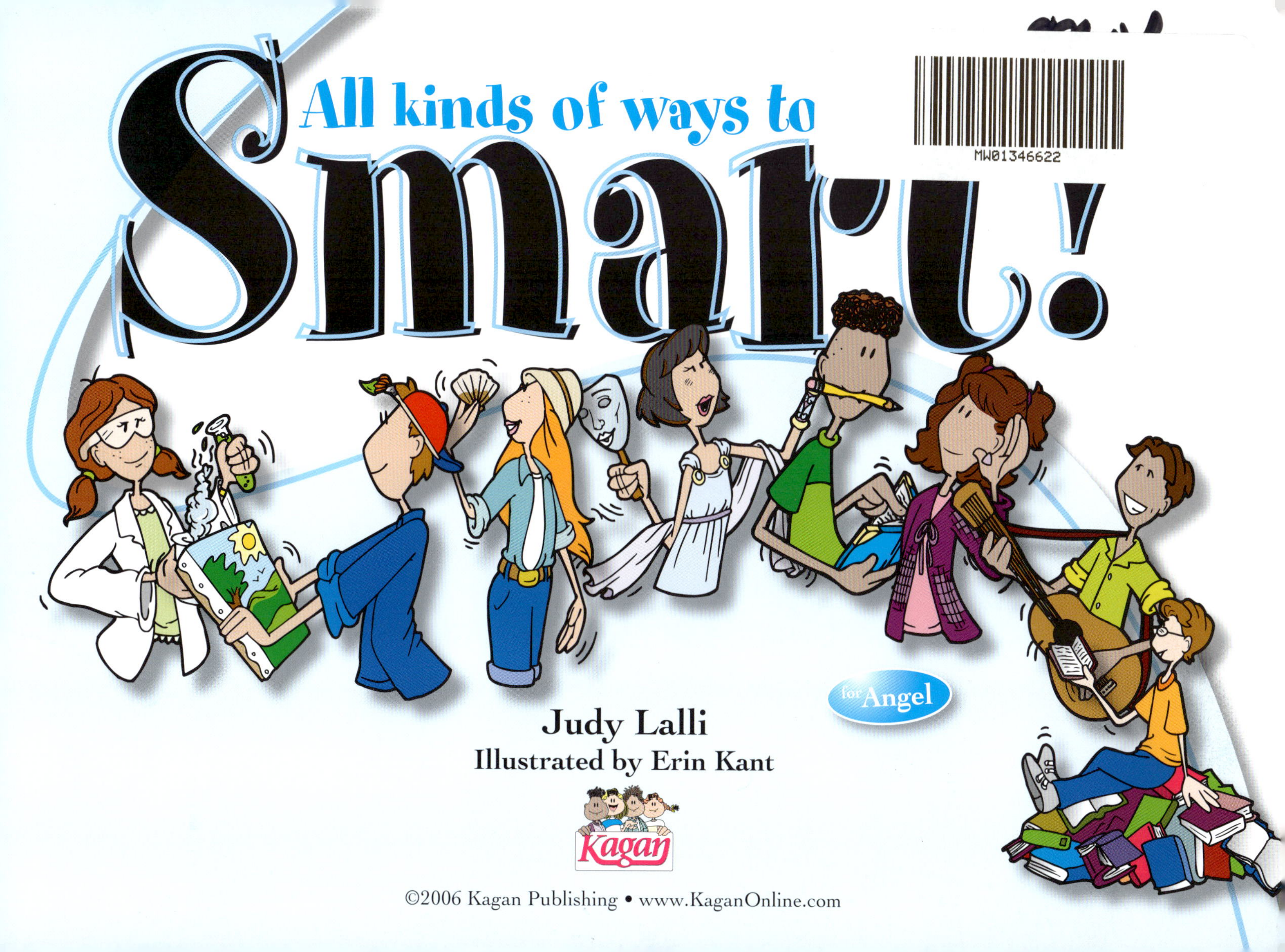
All kinds of ways to
Smart!
MW01346622
for Angel
Judy Lalli
Illustrated by Erin Kant
Kagan
©2006 Kagan Publishing • www.KaganOnline.com

Curt imagines he's an author when he sits down to play.
He describes what his characters would do and say.

He loves reading stories, and he loves holding books.
He loves the way the library feels and looks.

He's always writing letters, and his friends like what he's said.
He memorizes poems, and he likes to hear them read.

He wants to try to speak the other languages he's heard.
He wants to know the meaning of every new word.

How is he intelligent? He's **Word Smart!**

There are all kinds of ways to be smart!

Logic Smart

Danielle's favorite subjects are science and math.
She likes to do experiments and take a new path.

She can figure out a puzzle or a code or a maze.
She thinks it's fun to look at things in many different ways.

Solving problems logically is how she often goes.
Patterns, charts, and diagrams display the facts she knows.

Categorize, computerize, and alphabetize:
These are skills she uses to organize.

How is she intelligent? She's **Logic Smart!**

There are all kinds of ways to be smart!

Picture Smart

Shane thinks in pictures; he can see them in his head.
He remembers illustrations from the books he's read.

He gets an idea and sketches as he goes.
He'd rather make a drawing than explain what he knows.

He loves creating projects; he loves all kinds of art.
He can visualize a puzzle when the pieces are apart.

He's focused on the graphics, when he plays computer games.
He remembers people's faces better than their names.

How is he intelligent? He's **PICTURE Smart!**

There are all kinds of ways to be smart!

Ashish is singing and whistling and tapping his feet.
He's humming a tune; he's feeling the beat.

When he learns information using rhythm and rhyme,
He remembers the facts for a very long time.

When there's music in the background, he wants to sing along.
He can usually identify a note that's wrong.

He loves creating jingles, or a rap, a song, a cheer.
There are melodies inside him that he always seems to hear.

How is he intelligent? He's **Music Smart!**

There are all kinds of ways to **be smart!**

Brianne's lying on the grass; she's checking out a bug.
She knows what seeds she planted and where each hole was dug.

The trips she likes the best are to a park, a trail, a zoo.
She loves to study animals and what they like to do.

She knows about the dinosaurs and when they were alive.
She knows how bees help flowers and how they make a hive.

She loves to make collections of shells or rocks she's seen.
She cares about the planet, and she works to keep it clean.

How is she intelligent? She's **Nature Smart!**

There are all kinds of ways to be smart!

Kim seems to learn better when she's moving around.
It's hard for her to keep both feet on the ground.

She's active and athletic; she can take things apart.
She's dramatic, she likes role-plays, and she can act out a part.

She gestures and she points; she wants to demonstrate.
Her body helps her communicate.

She's good at sports; she loves to run.
She'd rather do anything than watch it be done.

How is she intelligent? She's **Body Smart!**

There are all kinds of ways to **be smart!**

Jamal sets his own pace; he likes his own space.
He often thinks better in a quiet place.

He likes to work alone, and he stays on task.
He finds his own answers to the questions he asks.

He thinks about thinking and how he learns best.
He likes to set goals and pass his own tests.

He has very strong opinions, and he says them aloud.
He learns from his mistakes; his successes make him proud.

SSSSHHH

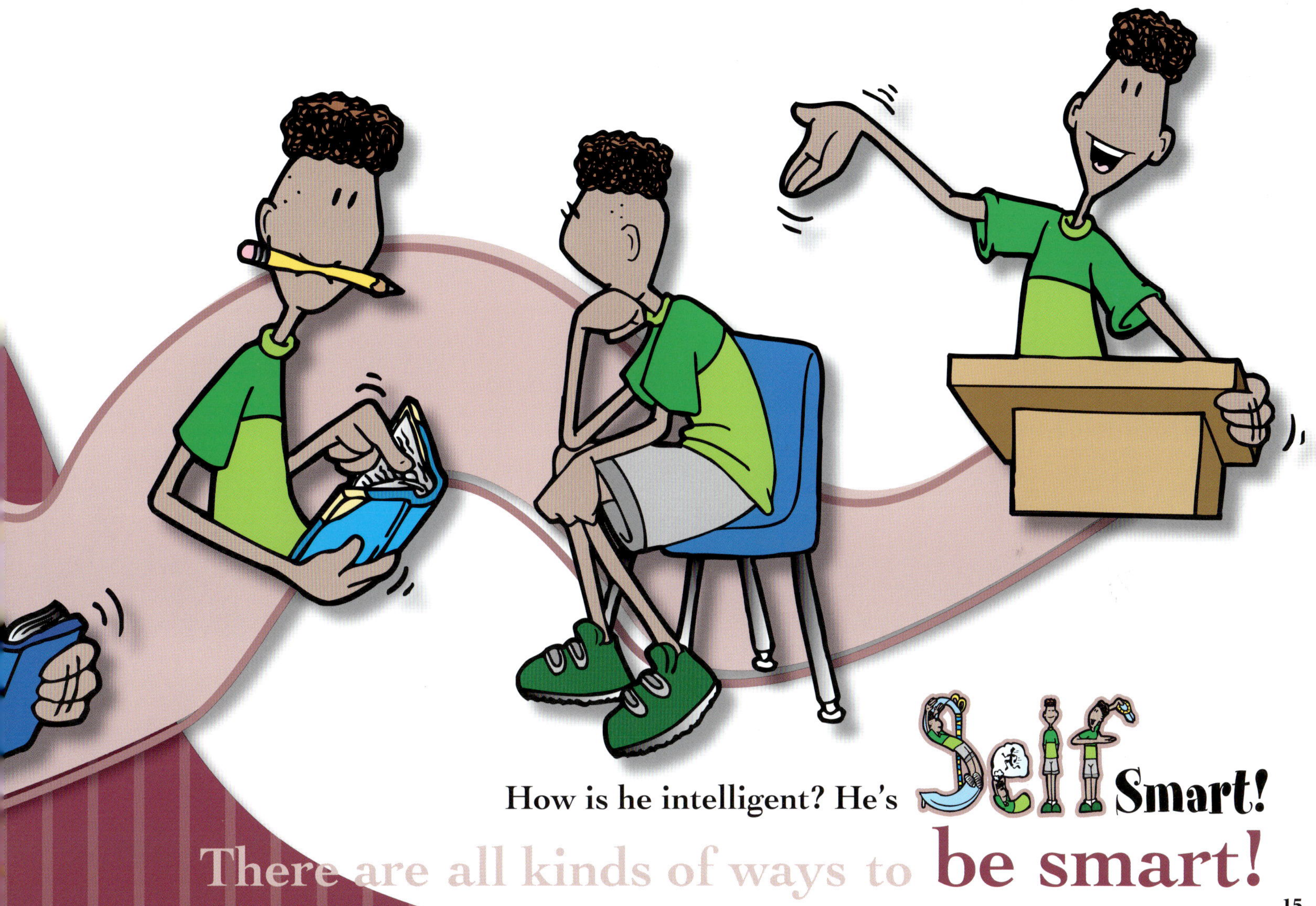

How is he intelligent? He's **Self Smart!**

There are all kinds of ways to be smart!

People Smart

Working in a group is how Rosa likes it done.
Sharing her ideas is part of the fun.

She's aware of other people and their feelings and moods.
She settles disagreements, arguments, and feuds.

She cooperates, collaborates, and likes to socialize.
She hears all points of view, and she sees all sides.

People see her as a leader; people ask her for advice.
People like it when she helps them, and that feels kind of nice.

How is she intelligent? She's **People Smart!**

There are all kinds of ways to be smart!

There are all kinds of

Curt loves to learn about words and their meanings.
He writes and he reads and learns poems by heart.

Danielle's good with numbers and thinking in patterns.
She loves to solve puzzles and take them apart.

Shane does his thinking in pictures and colors.
He learns best by drawing and studying art.

Ashish does his learning with music and rhythm.
There are all kinds of ways to **be smart!**

ays to be smart!

Brianne loves to learn about groupings in nature.
She can name and describe every plant on the chart.

Kim's into sports, and she learns best while moving.
She loves to perform and can play any part.

Jamal loves to think about new ways of learning.
He sets his own goals, and he can't wait to start.

SSSSHHH

Rosa learns best using teamwork and sharing.
There are all kinds of ways to **be smart!**

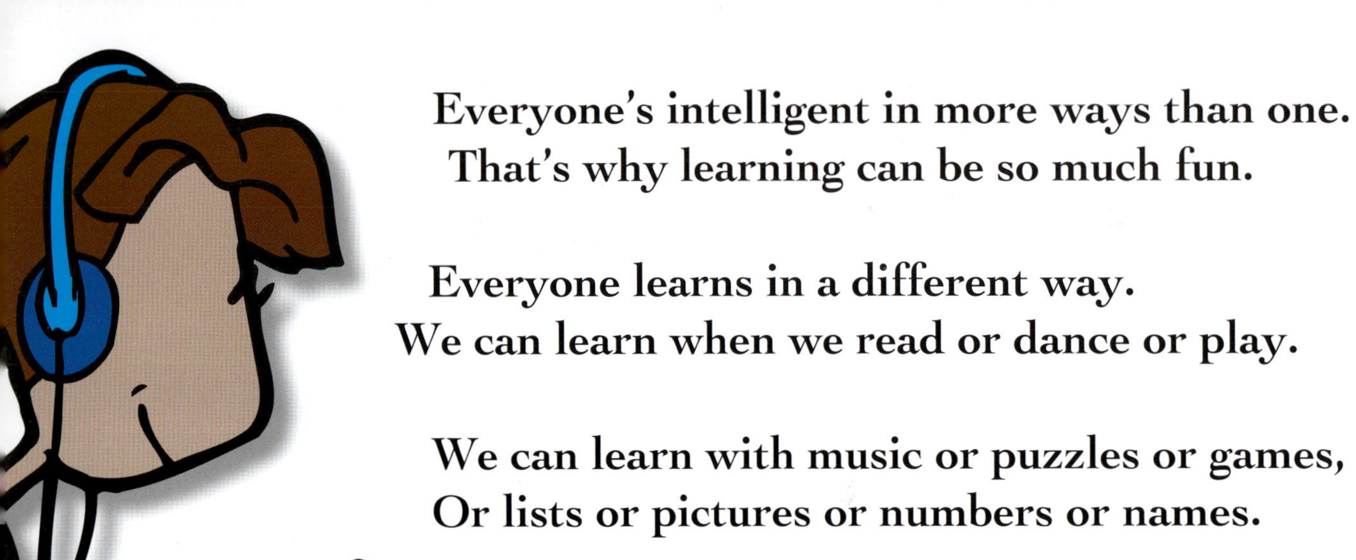

Everyone's intelligent in more ways than one.
That's why learning can be so much fun.

Everyone learns in a different way.
We can learn when we read or dance or play.

We can learn with music or puzzles or games,
Or lists or pictures or numbers or names.

There are lots of different ways to learn and think and do.
I'm smart in many ways, and so are you.

Whenever we share all the things we know,
We can help each other learn and grow.

And one thing I know in my heart:
There are all kinds of ways to **be smart!**